MotorSports

Snowmobile Racing

by William P. Mara

Consultant:
Ivan Hansen, Snowmobile Racer
and Member of the Board of Directors,
Midwest International Racing Association

CAPSTONE
HIGH/LOW BOOKS
an imprint of Capstone Press
Mankato, Minnesota

Capstone High/Low Books are published by Capstone Press
818 North Willow Street • Mankato, MN 56001
http://www.capstone-press.com

Library of Congress Cataloging-in-Publication Data
Mara, W. P.
    Snowmobile racing/by William P. Mara.
      p. cm.—(Motorsports)
    Includes bibliographical references (p. 46) and index.
    Summary: Introduces the sport of snowmobile racing, discussing the equipment
and tactics, race courses, necessary skills, and safety measures.
    ISBN 0-7368-0027-1
    1. Snowmobile racing—Juvenile literature. [1. Snowmobile racing.] I. Title. II. Series.
GV856.8.M37 1999
796.94—dc21   98-17221
                                               CIP
                                             AC

Editorial Credits
Michael Fallon, editor; Timothy Halldin, cover designer; Sheri Gosewisch, photo researcher

Photo Credits
Jason T. Griffiths, courtesy of CSRA, 26, 38, 42
Jay Ireland and Georgienne E. Bradley, 4, 24
Nick Devinck, courtesy of MIRA, cover, 20
Unicorn Stock Photos/A Ramey, 10, 12; Deneve Feigh Bunde, 34; Jeff Greenberg, 41
Valan Photos/Karen D. Rooney, 16
Visuals Unlimted/Steve Callahan, 18, 28
World Championship Snowmobile Derby, Eagle River, WI, 6, 9, 14, 22, 30, 33, 36

Table of Contents

Chapter 1

Snowmobiles

Snowmobiles are motorized sleds that can travel across snow and ice. Powerful engines drive snowmobiles. The engines are under hoods at the front of the snowmobiles. Snowmobiles are useful for doing work in the snow. People also ride snowmobiles for fun.

Snowmobiles are popular vehicles during winter. More than 2 million North Americans own snowmobiles. There are more than 220,000 miles (354,046 kilometers) of snowmobile trails in the United States and Canada. An average snowmobile travels more than 1,500 miles (2,414 kilometers) per year.

Snowmobile Manufacturers

Snowmobile use declined during the 1970s because of the energy crisis. Gasoline was expensive and in short supply. People stopped

In North America, snowmobiles are popular winter vehicles.

buying snowmobiles because the vehicles needed large amounts of gasoline to run.

Many snowmobile companies went out of business during the energy crisis. Today, only four companies make most of the snowmobiles in the world. Polaris and Arctco are in Minnesota. Ski-doo is in Quebec, Canada, and Yamaha is in Japan.

Manufacturers make snowmobiles for ordinary riders. But manufacturers also make some snowmobiles just for racers. Snowmobiles built for racing are very powerful. They also are very expensive. The average racing snowmobiles cost nearly twice as much as ordinary snowmobiles.

Snowmobiles have become popular since the energy crisis ended in the 1980s. Both children and adults enjoy riding snowmobiles. There are more than 3,000 clubs for snowmobilers in North America today.

Races in Winter
There are many snowmobile races each winter in the northern United States, Canada, and

Manufacturers make some snowmobiles just for racing.

some parts of Europe. Most snowmobile races feature only seven or eight drivers at a time. But other races can have up to 100 racers.

Many spectators attend snowmobile races. They watch the races from grandstands that surround the race tracks. Other people watch the races on television.

People in the cold-weather areas of the United States and Canada enjoy watching snowmobile races. People in Denmark, Norway, and Sweden also enjoy watching snowmobile races.

People in cold-weather areas of the United States and Canada enjoy watching snowmobile races.

Chapter 2

Snowmobile Racing History

In 1935, inventors tried to make the first motorized vehicles for traveling on snow. They mounted an engine on a sleigh. The engine powered gears under the sleigh. The gears turned a track that pushed the vehicle across the snow. But the motorized sleigh was too loud and too slow to be useful.

Inventors built the first real snowmobiles in the mid-1950s. Engines in the 1950s were smaller, quieter, and more powerful than in the 1930s. The inventors built small, light frames to hold the engines and tracks. These snowmobiles were not as slow and loud as the motorized sleigh. But the snowmobiles were dangerous because their engines were in the rear. The engines were open to the air and sometimes caught fire or exploded.

Inventors built the first real snowmobiles in the mid-1950s.

In the 1960s, manufacturers put snowmobile engines in the front and covered them with hoods.

Manufacturers improved snowmobiles in the 1960s. They built snowmobiles with lighter parts. They put engines in the front and covered the engines with hoods. The new snowmobiles were faster and safer than those of the 1950s.

Snowmobiles became popular among people who lived in cold climates. Mail carriers used snowmobiles to deliver letters and packages during winter. Doctors sometimes used snowmobiles to visit sick people. Rescue workers used snowmobiles to save people stranded in snow. People also started racing these early snowmobiles.

The First Snowmobile Races

People organized the first snowmobile races in northern Minnesota in the mid-1960s. The first races were cross-country races through the countryside. Cross-country races were the simplest way to race snowmobiles. The snowmobiles raced across open land to a finish line.

Snowmobile racing was popular in the early 1970s. People organized many different kinds of races. Race organizers built special arenas for races. Arenas were oval structures for sporting events. Spectators sat in rows of seats that surrounded the arenas. But fuel became expensive during the energy crisis. There were few snowmobile races during the late 1970s and early 1980s.

Snowmobile Racing Today

After the energy crisis, snowmobile racing became popular once again. Today, thousands of spectators attend races. The World Championship Snowmobile Derby in Eagle River, Wisconsin, draws more than 30,000 spectators each year.

There are many different kinds of snowmobile races. Hundreds of racers of all ages compete in official snowmobile races. Snowmobile racers compete on ice-oval race tracks and cross-country courses. Even children compete in races called Kitty Cat races.

The Midwest International Racing Association (MIRA), the Canadian Snowmobile Racing Association (CSRA), and International Snowmobile Racing (ISR) are organizations that sanction races. To sanction means to approve an event and make it official. Race organizers make the public aware of snowmobile races. They advertise races in magazines and on television.

Children compete in races called Kitty Cat races.

Chapter 3

Snowmobile Parts

S nowmobiles have many parts. Engines power tracks under snowmobiles. The tracks push the snowmobiles across the snow. Some parts help snowmobiles slide on the snow. Other parts help people steer snowmobiles.

Snowmobile racers sometimes have to fix their snowmobiles. They replace parts that are worn or broken. Most racers are good at fixing snowmobiles. They check the different parts of their snowmobiles for problems before every race.

Snowmobile Engines

Racing snowmobiles can have several kinds of engines. Some engines are bigger and more powerful than other engines. The smallest racing engine is the 440 fan-cooled engine.

Engines power tracks under snowmobiles.

Snowmobiles with these engines can reach speeds of 70 to 80 miles (113 to 129 kilometers) per hour.

Open-mod 1,000s are the largest and most powerful snowmobile engines. Snowmobiles with these engines can reach speeds of more than 100 miles (161 kilometers) per hour. The fastest speed for a snowmobile with an open-mod 1,000 is 152 miles (245 kilometers) per hour.

Snowmobile racers use throttles to accelerate. Racers change the speed of their snowmobiles by pressing throttle levers on their handlebars.

Steering

Snowmobile racers control their vehicles by using steering systems. The steering system is the pair of skis and handlebars located at the front of a snowmobile. Racers can turn the skis by turning the handlebars.

The skis are steel. The middle of the ski has a strip of strong metal called carbide. The

Snowmobile racers control their vehicles by using steering systems.

Snowmobiles have windshields in front to protect racers.

carbide strip is very sharp. It can cut easily through a top layer of snow or ice. This helps snowmobile drivers keep control of their vehicles.

Other Parts

There are other important parts on snowmobiles. Snowmobiles have seats. The seats have no seatbelts. Snowmobile racers often must stand up to go through jumps during races. The racers place their feet in footwells below and to the sides of their seats. Racers lock their feet in place under thin metal bars in the footwells.

Snowmobiles have parts that protect racers against snow spray and other objects. Snowmobiles often kick up bits of broken branches or rocks hidden under the snow. Shields cover the sides of snowmobile tracks to keep objects from flying up from them as they spin. Snowmobiles also have windshields in front to protect racers. The windshields keep most flying objects from hitting racers.

Engine

Seat

Footwell

Chapter 4

Snowmobile Racers

Snowmobile racers are usually between 18 and 35 years old. Most racers are men. But many women have started racing snowmobiles in recent years. Young people enjoy racing snowmobiles too.

Most people begin snowmobile racing by participating in small races near their homes. They enter larger, more challenging races as their skills improve.

Children begin racing in Kitty Cat races. Most Kitty Cat racers are between five and nine years old. Kitty Cat snowmobiles are smaller than adult models. The races are shorter and less dangerous.

Racing Abilities

People must have certain abilities to race snowmobiles. Snowmobile racers must be in

---

Many women have started racing snowmobiles in recent years.

good physical condition. Snowmobile racing is hard on the racers' bodies. Racers feel shock on their bodies when they land after jumps. Snowmobile engines are powerful and shake drivers' bodies. Racers sometimes take spills in their snowmobiles too.

Snowmobile racers must prepare their bodies for racing. They eat healthy foods and get plenty of sleep. They also exercise to build their physical condition and strength.

Strength is important in snowmobile racing. Racers must keep their snowmobiles under control. They drive their snowmobiles over jumps and through curves. The racers must control snowmobiles or they could fall off.

Snowmobile racers also need a good sense of balance. Racers must lean their bodies into turns. Their sense of balance helps them lean properly. Racers can flip their snowmobiles if they do not lean properly.

Racing Organizations

Most snowmobile racers belong to a racing organization called International Snowmobile

Racers drive their snowmobiles over many jumps and around many curves during races.

The best snowmobile racers have sponsors.

Racing (ISR). ISR sanctions snowmobile races and sets safety rules for the races. ISR also gives prizes to winners of snowmobile races. The Midwest International Racing Association (MIRA) is another organization that sanctions snowmobile races.

The best snowmobile racers have sponsors. Sponsors are businesses that pay a racer's expenses such as travel and racing equipment. Racers often use the sponsors' equipment or

put the sponsors' names on their snowmobiles
or racing uniforms. Most sponsors of
snowmobile racers are companies that make
snowmobiles and snowmobile equipment.

Many snowmobilers join clubs such as the
Vintage Snowmobile Club of America
(VSCA). Clubs hold events such as
snowmobiling trips and snowmobile shows.
Clubs also publish magazines that provide
members with information about snowmobiles
and snowmobile racing.

Chapter 5

Snowmobile Races

There are two main kinds of snowmobile racing. The most common kind takes place on cross-country race courses. Cross-country courses may have jumps and sharp curves. Most cross-country snowmobile race courses are in North America. Some are in Europe.

The other kind of snowmobile racing takes place on race tracks. Race organizers build snowmobile race tracks on snow or ice. They surround the tracks with grandstands for spectators.

Racing officials called flagmen use flags to signal important moments in a race. Both types of races begin when flagmen wave their green flags. Snowmobile racers rush from the starting line when the flagman waves the green flag. Racers drive as fast as possible in an attempt to win the race.

One kind of snowmobile race takes place on a race track.

During a race, the flagman uses flags of different colors to signal important moments. A red flag tells racers to stop because of an accident or other danger. A black flag tells racers that a racer has broken a racing rule. The racers stop until the flagman waves the green flag again. A white flag signals the last lap of a race. A checkered flag signals the end of a race.

The fastest three racers in a race receive trophies or ribbons. They also may earn prize money.

Races on Courses

Cross-country courses cover long stretches of snow-covered terrain. Terrain is the surface of the land. These courses can run through forests, mountains, and open fields. Some courses are more than 1,000 miles (1,609 kilometers) long.

Up to 100 snowmobile racers may take part in a cross-country race. Race organizers mark cross-country courses with flags or barrels so the racers know where to go. Organizers also give racers maps of the course.

A checkered flag signals the end of a snowmobile race.

Hill-climb races also take place on open terrain. The courses are on the slopes of steep, snow-covered hills or mountains. The snow on these courses is about two feet (.6 meters) deep. Hill-climb racers race to the top of the courses one at a time. Racers who reach the top in the shortest time win the hill-climb races.

Snowmobile racers sometimes cannot make it to the top of a hill-climb course. Their snowmobiles may not have enough power to reach the top. Or racers may not be able to hold onto their snowmobiles on the steep, uphill course.

Races on Tracks

There are many different types of snowmobile track races. Each type has its own race track.

The race tracks for snowmobile drag races are straight. They can be from around 600 feet (183 meters) to one-quarter mile (402 meters) long. The surfaces of the drag race tracks are usually ice. But the surfaces also may be grass or asphalt. Asphalt is a hard material people use to cover roads.

The race tracks for snowmobile drag races are straight.

Ice-oval racing takes place on icy, oval-shaped race tracks.

Four snowmobile racers compete against each other in each drag race heat. The fastest two racers in one heat advance to the next heat. The racers continue racing in heats until the last race of the four fastest competitors. The fastest racer in the final heat is the winner of the event.

Ice-oval racing takes place on icy, oval-shaped race tracks. Walls surround the

tracks. The tracks' curves are on slopes.
Snowmobile racers can drive fast and still stay
upright when they go into curves on ice-oval
race tracks. Seven or eight racers compete at
one time in ice-oval races. The races last
about 40 laps.

Le Mans races also take place on race
tracks made of snow or ice. Le Mans race
tracks have one long straightaway with curves
at both ends. The second side of the race
course has many sharp curves and jumps in it.
The race track curves are flat. This sometimes
causes racers to flip their snowmobiles on
the tracks.

Chapter 6

Snowmobile Safety

The first snowmobile racers did not need much safety gear. Early snowmobiles were not as fast as modern ones. The drivers did not crash their snowmobiles very often. They wore helmets, gloves, and goggles. Goggles are glasses that protect the eyes.

Snowmobile racers today take many safety precautions. They wear safety gear and check their snowmobiles carefully. They make sure their snowmobiles operate properly.

Improvements in Snowmobile Safety

In 1973, the Snowmobile Safety and Certification Committee (SSCC) made rules to protect snowmobile racers. The rules also protected ordinary snowmobile drivers. These rules are still in effect today. Good snowmobile drivers try to follow the SSCC's rules.

Snowmobile racers wear helmets and goggles to protect their heads and eyes.

The Snowmobile Safety and Certification Committee's first rule is that every snowmobile has to be checked regularly. SSCC officials check snowmobile brakes, lights, throttles, and engines. They also check snowmobile windshields and seats.

The SSCC's second rule is that beginning drivers must take snowmobile driving classes. Beginning drivers learn how to operate snowmobiles in these classes. They learn how to recognize dangerous weather conditions and learn what clothing to wear.

The SSCC also makes safety suggestions for experienced drivers. SSCC officials suggest that drivers keep their snowmobiles on trails. Snow can hide many dangerous objects during winter. Snowmobilers who drive off trails can hit hidden fences, barbed wire, and tree stumps. Snowmobile drivers should travel only at safe speeds or they could crash their vehicles.

SSCC officials also suggest that snowmobile drivers travel in groups. Drivers should take a friend who can go for help in dangerous situations. Snowmobile drivers also should

Snowmobile racers sometimes crash their snowmobiles during races.

learn hand signals that tell other riders when there is danger. Snowmobilers should stay off lakes and rivers even if the ice looks thick enough to ride on. The ice on lakes and rivers is sometimes not as thick as it looks. A snowmobile can fall through thin ice.

The rules for ordinary snowmobile drivers also apply to racers. Snowmobile racers sometimes crash their snowmobiles during races. Racers must be careful when racing to

Snowmobile racers wear safety vests to protect their chests, stomachs, and spines.

follow safety rules and stay on paths. Racers also must wear proper clothing and safety equipment when they race.

Safety Equipment for Racers

Snowmobile racing organizers require racers to wear safety equipment. Snowmobile racers must wear safety vests. Safety vests have strong plastic in them. They protect the racers' chests, stomachs, and spines. Snowmobile racers also wear elbow and knee pads. They wear thick gloves to protect their hands.

Snowmobile racing safety equipment has improved over the years. Helmets now protect racers' heads from serious blows. The shape of the helmets lessens the force of blows to the racers' heads. Face shields on helmets protect racers' eyes. Manufacturers make face shields from hard, clear plastic. Bodysuits protect racers' skin from harm during crashes.

In the past, snowmobile racers could not turn off their snowmobiles if they crashed. This was dangerous because the snowmobiles could run over the racers if they fell off.

Snowmobiles now have tether kill switches. These devices shut off engines if drivers crash. Each tether kill switch has a rope that attaches to a racer's wrist. The rope pulls the kill switch when the racer falls from the snowmobile. The switch shuts off the engine.

Improved safety equipment allows racers to enjoy their sport with less risk of serious injury. Snowmobile racers wear safety gear and follow safety rules so they can keep racing.

Words to Know

accelerate (ak-SEL-uh-rate)—to speed up

asphalt (ASS-fawlt)—a hard material used to cover roads

carbide (KAR-bide)—a strong metal

cross-country race (KROSS KUHN-tree RAYSS)—a race that runs through the countryside

face shield (FAYS SHEELD)—a hard, clear plastic shield on a helmet; a face shield protects a racer's eyes.

flagman (FLAG-man)—a racing official who uses flags to signal important events during a race

race course (RAYSS KORSS)—a path for racing through open terrain

race track (RAYSS TRAK)—a path or road people build for racing

sanction (SANGK-shuhn)—to approve an event and make it official

sponsor (SPON-sur)—a person or business that helps pay a racer's expenses

tether kill switch (TETH-ur KILL SWICH)—a device that shuts off an engine if the driver crashes

terrain (tuh-RAYN)—the surface of the land

throttle (THROT-uhl)—a device that controls a vehicle's speed

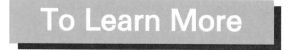
To Learn More

You can read articles about snowmobiles and snowmobile racing in the following magazines:

American Snowmobiler
Recreational Publications, Woodbury, Minn.

Hot Sled
Hot Sled Magazine, Missisauga, Ontario, Canada

Snow Goer
Ehlert Publishing Group, Inc., Minnetonka, Minn.

Snowmobile
Ehlert Publishing Group, Inc., Minnetonka, Minn.

Supertrax International
Supertrax Publishing, Mt. Albert, Ontario, Canada

Useful Addresses

**International Snowmobile Manufacturers
 Association**
1640 Haslett Road, Suite 170
Haslett, MI 48840

**International Snowmobile Racing
 Hall of Fame**
4302 Lake Shore Drive
Wausau, WI 54401

Internet Sites

**International Snowmobile Manufacturers
 Association**
http://www.snowmobile.org

The Snowmobile Homepage
http://www.sledding.com

The Vintage Snowmobile Club of America
http://www.vsca.com

Index